GOAL SETTING (LITERALLY)

WRITER CHAPS

SHORT BOOKS FULL OF OUTSTANDING ADVICE FROM AUSTRALIA'S TOP SPECULATIVE FICTION WRITERS

Season One

You Are Not Your Writing and Other Sage Advice, Angela Slatter

From Baby Brain To Writer Brain: Writing Through A World of Parenting Distractions, Tansy Rayner Roberts

Eyes on the Stars: Writing Science Fiction & Fantasy, Sean Williams

The Martial Art of Writing and Other Essays, Alan Baxter

Capturing Ghosts on the Page, Kaaron Warren

Headstrong Girl: How To Live A Writer's Life, Kim Wilkins

Season Two

What To Do When You Don't Have A Book Coming Out & Even More Sage Advice, Angela Slatter

Wide Open Fear, Lisa L. Hannett

Goal Setting (Literally), Lee Murray

GOAL SETTING (LITERALLY)

A Writer's Guide

Writer Chaps
Book 9

LEE MURRAY

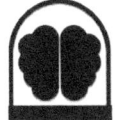

Brain Jar Press
PO Box 6687
Upper Mt Gravatt, QLD, 4122
Australia
www.BrainJarPress.com

Copyright © 2022 by Lee Murray

The moral right of Lee Murray to be identified as the author of this work has been asserted.

All rights reserved. No part of this book may be reproduced in any form or by any electronic or mechanical means, including information storage and retrieval systems, without written permission from the author, except for the use of brief quotations in a book review.

Cover design by Peter Ball
Cover Image: *Man sitting in lighbulb with laptop*, MJGraphics/Shutterstock.

ISBN: 978-1-922479-89-1 (Ebook) | 978-1-922479-88-4 (Chapbook)

Contents

Introduction	1
Why Write?	4
What Does Literary Success Mean To You?	6
Barriers To Success	8
Attributes For Success	10
Goal Setting	12
Remind Me Why I'm Doing This	15
Accountability And Monitoring	17
Sum It Up In A Word	19
Afterword	27
Bonus Chapter	28
About the Author	29

Introduction

'Our goals can only be reached through a vehicle of a plan, in which we must fervently believe, and upon which we must vigorously act. There is no other route to success.' —Pablo Picasso

Anything complex requires planning. As I write this introduction, my daughter is planning her wedding. Our kitchen table is covered in lists of friends and family to invite, photographers to contact, menu plans, invitation options, dress websites, and decorative choices. There is a lot to consider, and even with thoughtful planning, my daughter and her partner could still encounter problems. We've all seen the movies featuring wedding disasters: outdoor events conducted in the rain with dainty heels sinking in mud, flat tyres, delayed planes and other transport hiccups, hair fails, ketchup-stained dresses, feuding guests, double booked venues, and brides with cold feet. Any number of things might happen. But careful planning should allow our daughter and her partner to bring together the necessary expertise, and also identify contingencies, so they get the wedding they want, and a magical start to their future life together.

The same principle should apply to your literary career. Just as we wouldn't dream of holding a wedding without a plan, a great literary career also requires thoughtful planning. As Benjamin Franklin so famously said, 'By failing to prepare, you are preparing to fail.' There are plenty of failed writers. This workbook will help you avoid that calamity, providing a simple template for you to establish a set of customised fit-to-purpose literary goals. It takes just an hour or two to complete, and if carried out diligently, it should set you on a path to success, *as it applies to you*. Using this planner should also prevent you wasting time on roads that don't lead to your desired destination, because as philosopher Yogi Berra so rightly said, 'If you don't know where you are going, you'll end up someplace else.'

Why should you believe me? I've presented this template to various writers and writers' groups (both locally and internationally) over a number of years, and the feedback I've received suggests this system works. Authors, including award-winning and bestselling authors, who have used this little template have gone on to achieve literary success, some repeating this exercise more than once. More importantly, I have used this system for more than a decade and have found it to be a valuable tool for progressing my own literary career, helping me to become a multi-award-winning author of more than a dozen novels, two collections, sixteen anthologies, and more than seventy published novellas, short stories, and poems, as well as allowing me to serve the writing community as a literary judge, conference convenor, manuscript assessor, commissioning editor, and mentor. Using this chapbook as a template, there's no reason why you couldn't also achieve your version of literary success.

Using This Chapook

Goal Setting (Literally) offers targeted questions to help you determine what literary success means to you, and the steps you might undertake to achieve that vision. It takes just an hour or two to complete, which means you are only an afternoon away from creating a concrete record of your literary plan for the coming year and beyond, including practical, actionable, flexible goals to set you on the road to becoming the writer you want to be. As YA fantasy author, Sharon Manssen (*The Realm Trilogy*), states, 'completing this little workbook might just be the most productive hour you spend all year'.

Since your goals are personal to you, aim to complete each section of this chapbook on your own. However, consider getting together with a group of friends or colleagues and share your answers, as other people's reflections can be insightful. A robust discussion can help you to focus on what success looks like for you, identify any barriers and possible solutions, and develop targeted practical goals. Being willing to share your commitment with others can also help keep you accountable as you work towards your dream.

So, let's jump in.

Why Write?

From baking to basket weaving, batik to ballet, there are any number of creative activities we might engage in. So why choose writing? When I asked this question at my local writers' group, the answers were varied. We write for myriad reasons, including to engage, inform, and entertain readers. Reader response was another important motivation, and several authors said they wrote for the spontaneous joyous feedback they received from children. There's nothing like learning you're a child's favourite author or opening the post to discover a crayon drawing from a tiny fan reader. Inspiring a love of story and reading is a magical feeling, as is keeping someone up all night reading. Or offering an escape from the everyday. One emerging writer in our group mentioned a teacher who'd insisted she'd never amount to much, and whom she was now hell bent on proving wrong. Clearly, revenge can be a strong motivation! Several people cited gaining the approval or respect of a parent, grandparent, mentor, or a child as a key impetus. One person said they liked the opportunity to add new skills. Professional writers needed to make money from their work.

Sometimes, we're trying to improve our skills, so we can write better communications in our day jobs, or in our personal life.

Other reasons included: I can't help it; for my wellbeing; to have a voice; to record family memories for posterity; to write the stories I want to read; or tell the story I'm burning to tell. All of these reasons are valid.

Exercise One: Why Write?

Why do you choose to write? List ALL the reasons. Nothing is too ridiculous.

What Does Literary Success Mean to You?

This question often surprises, but literary success means different things for different people. If your reasons for writing include fame and fortune then, for you, signing a book-to-film contract might represent the ultimate in literary success. Or perhaps you'd like to see an orange Amazon bestseller banner associated with your book. You might dream of snagging a high-profile literary agent, or a large advance. An invitation to speak at a literary event. A story commission by a top editor.

On the other hand, if you're an emerging writer, literary success might be as simple as having a colleague introduce you as a writer in a social group or event. You might have mastered a new writing technique, tried your hand at a new form, uncovered a good research site or tool, or discovered how to use the editing tools in Word. Success might have been as small as coming up with a good title for a piece of writing, learning to format your work like a professional, or pressing SUBMIT on a piece for publication.

It might also mean expanding your network of creatives and industry professionals through the organisation of a literary event, participation in a critique group, or collaboration with another creative. Often, a writer's biggest achievement will have been completing a manuscript. As my US colleague, horror-suspense author Josh Malerman (*Bird Box*, *Unbury Carol*), writes:

> 'I live by a rule of "no Vs". [Regarding] any success beyond the act of actually finishing a book, I allow no sense of Validation, Vindication, Victory, or Vengeance. I'm not out to prove anybody wrong (tempting as that may often be). Finishing is always enough. The dream. The rest, gravy.'

Exercise Two: Embrace Your Successes

Did you have any successes last year? What were your positive literary moments? Anything that felt like a success, however small, write it down now. Brainstorm as many positives as you can. If you're struggling for ideas, you can download the responses of 80 of my writer friends here: http://BrainJarPress.com/GoalSettingBonus

.

Barriers To Success

Perhaps you had some goals last year and, for some reason, you didn't accomplish them. In 2020-2021, the global COVID-19 pandemic disrupted many writers. Thrown into repeated lockdowns, with job loss, financial stress, work-from-home and home-schooling demands, and struggles with anxiety, uncertainty, and grief, many writers were forced to re-evaluate their literary goals.

Even without the pandemic, life can throw us curve balls. Perhaps the skills course you planned to take was discontinued, or the cost of attending a convention was too high. Attempts to secure a literary agent failed. The story you submitted to a major magazine was rejected. The clauses in the publishing contract weren't in your favour.

Very often, these things are outside our control. Occasionally, though, the barriers to success are internal. Sometimes, we sabotage ourselves, or we get off track, focussing on tasks which may not lead us to our desired outcome. In my own career, I learned early on that sharing critiques with other writers helped me to analyse and understand their writing techniques, play a role in shaping their work, and receive helpful comments for tightening my own fiction. This seemed like a win-win to me, so I threw myself into various writing and critique groups, offering to share work with lots of different creatives. Over time, I gained a reputation as a strong assessor and editor of genre fiction, one colleague referring to me as 'Lee-the-Knife' for the way I trimmed and tightened her work. These editing and story development skills led to wonderful new opportunities for me as an anthologist, commissioning editor, literary judge, and writing mentor, all roles I love.

How is that a barrier? While these roles are hugely rewarding, committing to these tasks steals time from my core goal of becoming the best *author* of genre fiction I can be, something I can't achieve if I am writing less and editing more.

Exercise Three: Barriers To Success

Identify the barriers that may have prevented you achieving literary success and write them down here. Be HONEST.

Exercise Four: Brainstorm Solutions

Consider your list of barriers. Brainstorm solutions for overcoming these roadblocks. Write down as many solutions as you can.

Attributes For Success

When developing our goals, it can be helpful to examine the qualities of successful people you admire. These people don't necessarily have to be writers: they might be sportspeople, community leaders, musicians, or even friends or family members. What specific qualities do they embody which contribute to their success? Are these people confident, driven, dynamic? Perhaps the person you admire is an especially evocative speaker, or they take a practical can-do approach to problem solving. They might demonstrate high levels of energy. Or maybe they're highly productive as the result of effective time management skills. It can be useful to pinpoint key attributes of people you admire, and then when you're ready to develop your goals, include tasks and activities which will enable you to develop those same qualities, or at least *your version* of those qualities.

If you note that the person you admire is a confident effective speaker, for example, and you'd like to emulate that ability, your goal might be to participate in a toastmasters' club and develop your public speaking skills. If you admire someone for their methodical approach to problem solving, you might decide to investigate tools to help you in that area, such as learning to use flowchart and process software. To improve your own energy levels, you might write some goals around your sleep and dietary habits. The next exercise is an opportunity to explore the personal characteristics of successful people you admire as a way of informing your literary goal setting process.

Exercise Five: Attributes For Success

Imagine someone you admire and whom you consider successful, a writer or various writers... What attributes or qualities might have contributed to their success? Write a list.

Remember, the goal of this exercise is not to compare yourself to those people, as comparison can engender envy, which can have negative consequences. The point here is to reflect on the character traits which comprise your ideal of success.

Exercise Six: Character Development For Writers

What might you need to do in order to become more like the person you admire? What attributes, qualities, or skills will you need to acquire or perfect? Write a list.

Goal Setting

Now, that we've identified what success looks like for you, the obstacles that have prevented you from achieving that success in the past, and the characteristics you might need to foster in order to achieve success, we can establish a set of goals for you to work towards for the coming year.

Many of you will be familiar with the SMART system of goal setting which originated in the 80s and has been attributed to Management by Objectives visionary Peter Drucker. First cited by George T Doran in the November 1981 issue of *Management Review*, the SMART system refers to a set of criteria for creating goals. I like to use my own mnemonic, SPICE, which has similar criteria, but channels the lyrics of the nineties' pop band, the Spice Girls. This is simply to remind you that, as the song states, your literary goals should be created with the intent of getting you 'what you really, really, want'.

SPICE Goals

Using the SPICE mnemonic, each goal you create should be:

- Specific (simple and significant)
- Practical (with actionable tasks and attainable outcomes)
- Immediate (written in present and not future tense, where possible)
- Constrained (make your goal time-based by setting a deadline or deadlines)
- Earnest (your goals should contribute to *your* version of literary success).

Sometimes, creating one goal might lead to another. For example, if you're a new writer and your initial vision of literary success is seeing your first publication in a well-known magazine, then your goal might be to check out the magazine's submission guidelines and undertake all the technical steps necessary to submit your work. This might mean getting into the habit of formatting your stories in Shunn Modern style[1], learning how to remove identifying material from your files, and signing up for a Submittable account.[2] For your goal to be effective, you should set a prescribed timeframe to undertake these tasks.

However, if your ultimate measure of literary success is to achieve the Pulitzer Prize, don't write that down, since you have no guarantee of ever obtaining that coveted prize. It's great to aim high, but for the majority of us, winning a Pulitzer isn't simple or readily attainable. More importantly, a goal like that is, for the most part, out of our control. Instead, focus on goals which might bring you *nearer* to that Pulitzer possibility. For example, in the next six months, you might undertake to complete a plotting course which will allow you to create the planning blueprint for the high-quality ground-breaking novel *worthy of* a Pulitzer. Or, in the next month, you might undertake a comprehensive search of the publishing houses whose authors have appeared on the Pulitzer longlists for the last five years, analysing those works to gain a clear understanding of the kinds of literature those houses publish, and identifying any gaps that might exist in their stables. Neither of these goals will gain you the Pulitzer, but you'll have acquired valuable skills and information which might get you closer to that endpoint. So, sometimes, the trick is to choose a series of *attainable* goals that will move you as close as you can to your personal vision of literary success.

Exercise Seven: Goal Setting

List at least TEN firm goals that you will undertake in the next year in order to become the writer you want to be using the SPICE mnemonic. Rank your goals in order of priority.

Exercise Eight: Goal Sequencing

Which of your goals are big-picture long-term goals? Which are bite-sized short-term goals?

List your goals in chronological order. Note the deadlines in your calendar.

---

1. Guidelines available online at https://www.shunn.net/format/story/
2. Submittable is a submissions management system used by many publishers and magazines. Find out more about it here: https://www.publishersweekly.com/pw/by-topic/digital/Apps/article/81253-submittable-comes-of-age.html

Remind Me Why I'm Doing This

'Our goals can only be reached through a vehicle of a plan, in which we must fervently believe, and upon which we must vigorously act. There is no other route to success.' —Pablo Picasso

'Everything is created twice, first in the mind and then in reality.' —Robin Sharma

For many of us, writing our goals is difficult, yet if we are to turn our dreams into reality, planning is just the beginning. Now that we've determined what we need to do to set us on the path to success, we need to knuckle down and carry out the prescribed tasks. There is no point in setting goals if you have no intention of acting upon them – you may as well wait for a fairy godmother to come along and wave her magic wand. While some writers may indeed benefit from a magical stroke of luck, sadly those instances are rare. Most of us are better served with some well-designed goals carried out with diligence and verve.

Well-conceived goals, when acted upon, can prevent you

from getting distracted and wasting time on other less vital tasks. In short, they give you direction, and get you there faster.

For several years, I lived in Wisconsin in the United States. In the fall, I would gaze out the window, watching the activities of the chipmunks in my yard. We don't have chipmunks in New Zealand, so I was always fascinated by their industry and their energy, the tiny animals carrying nut after nut across the lawn and up to a hollow in a tree to save for the winter. But chipmunks tend to lack focus, so often when they saw a new nut, they would drop the nut already in their cheeks, in favour of the new one. Sometimes, they would exchange their nut four or five times before they would finally climb the tree to stash the nut in their storehouse. The chipmunks had a clear goal (to store food in preparation for the winter), but they wasted valuable fair-weather time 'tasting' each new nut they encountered, an activity which distracted them from their goal.

> 'The trouble with not having a goal is that you can spend your life running up and down the field and never score.' —Bill Copeland

Accountability And Monitoring

Now that you have established some goals and created a timeline for completing the work, it's important to refer to these checklists regularly to ensure you haven't gone off track, or even to revise a goal or two should external forces mean that achieving your original deadlines is no longer possible. Create a handy portable record of your goals to carry with you in your bag, or in the glove box of the car. Or copy your goals into the note function of your phone, so you can refer to them as required. You might also like to share your goals with a trusted friend or colleague who will (kindly) hold you accountable. If you worked through this book in a group of fellow writers, then you might like to set a date to reconvene and update each other on your progress.

In summary:

- Keep your goals on hand for easy reference.
- Revisit your goals regularly (and set dates to monitor your progress).
- Share your goals with others for improved accountability.

- Adjust or refine you goals if need you need to.

Wait? I can adjust my goals? Yes, it's important to keep in mind that it can, occasionally, become necessary to revise or update our goals. For example, we may discover that a goal we created is taking us off in an unintended direction, or we need more time to master a skill than we had initially anticipated. On the other hand, if the task is easier than expected, we might extend our goal to complete additional tasks. There are times when we will come up against unexpected roadblocks, an event cancelled for reasons outside our control, for example. And sometimes life gets in the way and our priorities change. A sick parent or child, a house move, a relationship breakdown, or a new job are the kinds of events which can disrupt even the most robust planning. If you are certain that you are changing your goals for valid reasons (and the change is not a form of self-sabotage or procrastination), then it is perfectly reasonable to adjust your goals. Be kind to yourself.

Remember:

- 'There are no mistakes in life, only lessons. There is no such thing as a negative experience, only opportunities to grow, learn and advance along the road of self-mastery.' —Robin Sharma
- 'Everything in the world was made up by people that were no smarter than you.' —Steven Jobs
- Stuff happens.
- Work hard to know what you don't know.
- Take time to get it right in the beginning.
- Never forget why you started.

Sum It Up In A Word

Another helpful shortcut for occasions when you might not have your goals on hand is to find a single word that encompasses your goals for the year. That way, when you're confronted with a new project or task, you can very quickly decide if the new direction fulfils or distracts from your purpose. While it doesn't replace the hard work of goal setting, it does provide a simple and effective decision-making tool. As an example, here are some of the words I selected to sum up my annual goals over the past decade.

Wanderlust

This was a word choice from early in my writing career, intended to reflect my passion for writing and my intent to challenge myself to write in as many genres and formats as I could, to explore various writing styles and approaches so I might discover what most excited me, and to seek out new opportunities. This word goal meant that, over the course of the year, I challenged myself to write widely and with abandon and passion, experiencing new forms and genres and investing in new communities. Having this concept in my head encouraged me to learn new skills, meet new people, and attend conventions, conferences, and presentations. The word 'wanderlust' might not be helpful if your goal is to make a name in the steampunk genre, or if you wish to maximise your income (which can require more focus), but for a writer on the cusp of her writing career, 'wanderlust' provoked a time of playful exploration, encapsulating my intent.

Blockbuster

I think the essence of this word is somewhat self-explanatory. I chose the word 'blockbuster' around six or seven years into my writing career. At this point, I had invested deeply in my writing skills, including participating in numerous professional development opportunities. I was heavily involved in writing communities and community-related projects, and I had written three novels. It was time to bring it up a notch. With the word 'blockbuster' firmly entrenched in my head, I looked for a gap in the market, searching works by my favourite authors for a subject and genre which hadn't yet been fully exploited. When I hit on an idea that made my blood sing (I was out doing a long-distance run in the forest with some friends when I had that eureka moment), I went straight home, labelled my file 'Global Blockbuster', and set about writing. The result was *Into the Mist*, a speculative military thriller set in the dense New Zealand bush, and incorporating local mythology, lore, and culture. While I was writing the book, I went back to my reading list for publishers of similar titles, investigating the publishing houses that had released those works in case they might also be a good fit for my work. I stumbled across an excellent press that was publishing some of my favourite authors, and I kept my eye on them for about a year. When they opened a submission call, I was ready with my new novel and my query letter. Although the press had no knowledge of me or my writing, the turn-around time from submission to contract was just nine days. The first Taine McKenna adventure was underway. Interestingly, while the book has never a *global* blockbuster, it has been the break-out novel of my career and remains my best-selling book to date, exceeding all others in the publisher's stable in its first year of publication. The book went on to win New Zealand's Julius Vogel Award for Best Novel, was and long listed for the Bram Stoker Award®. The publisher immediately demanded a sequel, something I hadn't even considered. Not only that, because I was part of the publisher's stable, I was rubbing shoulders with some of my writing idols, many of whom have since been instrumental in supporting my career. The reverberations from that single word (and the work it engendered) have been extraordinary.

Of course, there is an element of luck in all these things – the publishing industry is fickle and cantankerous at the best of times, and many excellent works never make it to publication – but I do sometimes wonder if my word for the year hadn't been 'blockbuster' whether I would have achieved those same outcomes.

Souche

Still later in my career, I selected the word 'souche' which is a French term meaning root, stump, or trunk, and also comprises the notions of ancestry, heritage, or origins. With this word, I went back to basics, honing my skills and consolidating on my growing brand as a New Zealand horror-thriller writer whose works draw heavily on local lore and landscape. This married well with my emerging identity as a Kiwi writer. At the time, I was writing *Into the Sounds*, the sequel to *Into the Mist*; tricky since I hadn't written the first book with a sequel in mind, and I was scrambling to pull a long story arc from exiting story threads. The idea inherent in the word 'souche' kept me on track, enabling me to complete the project, while also establishing me as a writer of New Zealand-centric genre fiction.

Kindness

To me kindness is a vital characteristic of a successful writer. When I consider authors I admire, the key characteristic that stands out for me is their generous support of other writers. Choosing the word 'kindness' was my attempt to pay back some of the support shown to me by the writing community. So, over this particular year, I took on mentoring projects, critiqued new writers, gave presentations, appeared in schools, co-ordinated community projects, and programmed conventions. Wherever I could offer help, I put my hand up. It was frantic year, but also a rewarding one. Not only did I gain new skills from these projects, but I was also able to grow my network of writing colleagues and industry professionals. I created a community around me, with some of those people becoming lifelong friends. Although kindness is no longer my annual word choice, it remains fundamental to my identity as a writer.

No!

After my year of kindness, I realised I was wearing myself thin, taking on too many projects and leaving little or no time for my own writing. Clearly, I'd done a great job embracing the concept and establishing myself as a writer who supported other writers, because I was inundated with requests for help, often from people I'd never met. Could I read and edit a manuscript for free? Could I run a series of workshops? Could I provide a list of publishers? Or reviewers? Or bloggers? Or authors? Could I help with a query letter?

I invested thousands of volunteer hours in other people's literary projects. Even now, some years after selecting the word 'kindness', I receive numerous requests for help among my messages every day. I love supporting people and getting a sneak peek at their projects, but by the end of my year of kindness, I was in danger of breaking down; kindness was derailing my own writing. The following year, I decided on the word 'no' to remind myself not to take on extraneous projects that would rob me of my writing time. I still helped where I could, but for a time, at least, I was more selective about my choices.

Whittle

The word 'whittle' is another word choice that reflects my intent to focus my efforts on projects which inspire me. For me, this means whittling down my community volunteer hours to manageable levels, while also whittling away at my personal goals like a sculptor or carver, shaping and creating works by either by building on or completing existing projects.

Finally, while I haven't yet done this, you might also select a metaphor, idiom, or phrase to represent your plan for the year. 'Fortune favours the bold', 'free spirit', 'where there's a will there's a way', and 'ahead of the curve' are possibilities.

Exercise Nine: Sum It Up In A Word

Consider the 250 words and phrases below. If one of these encapsulates your intent for the year, underline or highlight it. If none of these words resonate, come up with one of your own. Write it here:

abandon, abundance, acceptance, accomplish, achieve, acknowledgement, advance, adventure, art, attain, attempt, attitude, authenticity, author, balance, basic, belonging, bestseller, blockbuster, book, brave, breadth, break-out, calibre, challenge, character, chicken, clarity, collaborative, commit, communicate, community, compassion, complete, complex, constructive, considered, consolidate, continue, convention, courage, craft, create, cultivate, custom, dedication, deliver, desire, development, digital, direction, dramatic, dream, effective, effort, eloquent, encourage, energy, engage, engender, enhance, enjoy, enough, entertain, envelope, escape, evidence, evolution, excellence, experiment, explode, fantasy, fast-track, favourite, fearless, feature, feedback, ferocious, finesse, finish, fire, first principles, focus, force, foreshadow, forgiveness, forward, freedom, fulfilment, full-time, game, gem, generate, gratitude, grit, groceries, growth, happiness, harvest, heart, heroic, health, honesty, humanity, identity, imagination, immersive, improvement, inclusion, incremental, individual, inform, initiative, innovative, insight, inspire, integrity, interact, journey, killer, kind, knowledge, learning, loud, lucid, lucrative, mentor, meteoric, methodical, milestone, mission, moxie, mystery, network, nightmare, novelist, nurture, oceanic, opportunity, order, outreach, panache, pantser, patient, pay-it-forward, peaking, perfection, perform, persistence, pizzazz, plucky, poignant, polish, power, practical, practice, pragmatic, prelude, presence, proud, profitable, prolific, productive, professional, publishable, purpose, quality, questing, readability, readers, real, reciprocal, recognition, record, refine, reflective, regroup, representation, reputation, research, resilient, resolute, resonate, resourceful, respect, revamp, revise, reward, royalty, rules, safety, sanctuary, satisfaction, self, sensitivity, share, simplicity, smart, soul, sparkle, spirit, stamina, standard, statement, steady, stepwise, story arc, storytelling, straight and narrow, strategic, stride, structure, style, subversive, sufficient, surprise, theme, thread, tradition, transformative, trial, truth, ultimate, unconventional, undauntable, underpinning, understated, undertake, unfettered, unleash, unquiet, validation, variety, venture, verve, voice, voyage, wanderlust, web, wellbeing, whimsy, whittle, wrangler, writer, zest, zing.

Afterword

I hope you've found this goal setting exercise useful for reflecting on your writing career. If you've worked through the book as prescribed, you should have a better idea of what literary success means to you, a set of realistic actionable goals which will allow you to progress towards that vision over the next year, and dates and strategies to keep you accountable, so you're not chipmunking from task to task. And if you encounter a set-back, you'll know to reassess and refine your goals accordingly. For best results, revisit your core goals annually, as your vision of success will likely change over time. I wish you all the best for your literary career.

Bonus Chapter
LITERARY SUCCESS: MOVING GOAL POSTS

Writer friends, what does literary success look like to you?

Is it a book deal or commission, learning a new skill, a film option, an invitation to present at a conference, holding the book in your hand, being part of a critique group, feedback from a reader who isn't your mother, being brave enough to submit, mentoring another creative, finding a good title, or just discovering the read-aloud function on Word? In your view, what constitutes success?

To find out how seventy other authors answered these questions, download the Goal Setting (Literally) bonus chapter at http://BrainJarPress.com/GoalSettingBonus

About the Author

Lee Murray is an author, editor, and poet from Aotearoa New Zealand, and a USA Today Bestselling author. She is the winner of multiple Sir Julius Vogel, Australian Shadows, and Bram Stoker Awards, and is her country's only recipient of the Shirley Jackson Award for psychological horror. She has also been shortlisted for numerous other awards, including the Aurealis and British Fantasy Awards. Titles by Lee include military thriller series, the Taine McKenna Adventures, supernatural crime-noir trilogy The Path of Ra (with Dan Rabarts), and short fiction collection, *Grotesque: Monster Stories*. She is the editor of nineteen volumes of dark fiction, among them *Black Cranes: Tales of Unquiet Women* (with Geneve Flynn) and *Asian Ghost Short Stories* (Flame Tree Press), and she was named Lit Reactor's Editor of the Year for 2021. Other works by Lee include non-fiction title *Mark My Words: Read the Submission Guidelines and Other Self-editing Tips* with Angela Yuriko Smith, and several books for children. Her short stories and poems have appeared in prestigious venues such as *Weird Tales*, *Space and Time*, and *Grimdark Magazine*. She is a Rhysling- and Pushcart-nominated poet, and recently won an Australian Shadows Award for her poem "Cheongsam" which appeared in *Tortured Willows: Bent, Bowed, Unbroken*. A manuscript assessor, international literary judge, conference panellist and guest of honour, Lee is a former HWA Mentor of the Year, NZSA Honorary Literary Fellow, and a Grimshaw Sargeson Fellow. Read more at https://www.leemurray.info/

- facebook.com/lee.murray.393
- twitter.com/leemurraywriter
- instagram.com/leemurray2656
- bookbub.com/authors/lee-murray
- amazon.com/Lee-Murray/e/B0068FHSC4

Thank You For Buying This Brain Jar Press Chapbook

To receive special offers, bonus content, and info on new releases and other great reads, visit us online at www.BrainJarPress.com

www.ingramcontent.com/pod-product-compliance
Lightning Source LLC
Chambersburg PA
CBHW021454080526
44588CB00009B/849